AN INVITATION TO THE AWAKENING HEART

Communing With The Inner Teacher

– NICK DAVIS –

An environmentally friendly book printed and bound in England by
www.printondemand-worldwide.com

Mixed Sources
Product group from well-managed
forests, and other controlled sources
www.fsc.org Cert no. TT-COC-002641
FSC © 1996 Forest Stewardship Council

PEFC Certified
This product is
from sustainable
managed forests
and controlled
sources
PEFC www.pefc.org
PEFC/16-33-415

This book is made entirely of chain-of-custody materials

i

www.fast-print.net/store.php

An Invitation to the Awakening Heart –
Communing with the Inner Teacher
Copyright © Nick Davis 2013

A catalogue record for this book is available from the British Library

ISBN 978-178035-534-4

First published 2013 by
FASTPRINT PUBLISHING
Peterborough, England.

*To my beloved Anne, James and Emily
and to all my companions over the years
who have shared with me the path of
Miracles.*

Nick Davis

Who walks with me?

This question should be asked a thousand times a day, till certainty has ended doubting and established peace. Today let doubting cease.

God speaks for you in answering your question with these words:

'I walk with God in perfect holiness. I light the world. I light my mind and all the minds which God created one with me.'

A Course In Miracles

Nick Davis

Contents

Introduction

In 1984 I realised that I was seeking another teacher, one who could take me further on the pathway of learning the truth. I was answered with an invitation to study 'A Course In Miracles'. Through practicing the lessons of ACIM and teaching the lessons to others, so as to learn them more completely, I became able to hear a clear 'Voice' within my own mind.

In Part One of this book I share a brief account of my story with 'The Course' so far and I also share the framework of my life in which I listen to the Inner Teacher.

In Part Two some of the longer spontaneous communications I have had with the Teacher are shared. These have clarified for me concepts and ideas that are expressed in the Course, and with them comes a constant encouragement and invitation to do the lessons of the Workbook which are the means to find Inner Peace.

In Part Three I have introduced some of the questions that have come to me over the years, from the profound to the mundane, that have been answered by my loving companion.

I trust that in sharing the teachings I have received, it will encourage you to practice the simple inward listening in the stillness that will enable you to know 'Who walks with you'. In realising the Companionship of this One, you will learn, like me, that indeed, 'All is Well'.

Nick Davis, Worcester, June 2013

Part I

'I am here to be truly helpful…'

ACIM text p.28

In the Beginning...

I discovered 'A Course in Miracles' in March 1984, or maybe I should say it found me. I was living in Bournemouth in the South of England at the time running my own fitted furniture business. My business was however not my primary interest, the real excitement of my life was the study and teaching of the principles of Science of Mind, the inspiring writings of Ernest Holmes who founded Religious Science in the USA.

On one evening a week I would teach a class on Prosperity, Healing or Meditation at the Centre of Unity in Bournemouth. My Spiritual teacher Reverend Norah Boyd had retired in 1982, and I had taken up the mantle of teaching the thriving group she had gathered over the ten years of her ministry. In hindsight I realise that I was still seeking more and without voicing it, another teacher.

Early in 1984 when speaking to my dear friend Ron Eager, an accomplished spiritual healer who ran the Centre of Unity, he said he had discovered some books called 'A Course in Miracles' and that he felt they were for me. I took a look at them. They were big, blue and gold hardback volumes which were very impressive in quality and thickness. They came as a set of three. On opening them at random and reading a few paragraphs, I was put off by the overly Christian language of the text: words like sin and atonement were words I had tried to leave behind in my studies of psychology and the 'New Thought Teachings'. I handed them back with a polite, 'Thanks but no thanks, not for me'.

A few weeks later I was reading an article in the Science of Mind magazine, in my view one of the most inspiring, uplifting and positive magazines published on New Thought teachings, and in it was an article about 'The Course in Miracles' and how it made an impact on a number of Science of Mind students in a very inspiring way. Oh yes, I thought, they're those books that Ron showed me.

Shortly after this a letter arrived to our group from a Science of Mind minister Rev Burt Hodgkiss, who was travelling the world with his wife Nonnie. He was coming to Europe, would be in England and would love to introduce our group to a new teaching called 'A Course in Miracles'. Once, twice, three times now this had knocked on my door, maybe I needed to have a look at it I thought. With the agreement of Ron, the group and my fellow teacher of Science of Mind, Beryl Fuller, we invited Burt to do some days of teaching at the Centre of Unity.

We were in for a surprise and a treat. Far from being a conventional Christian, Burt arrived, cowboy hat on head, six feet four inches tall, a well broken nose, huge grin and beautiful petite blonde wife Nonnie. The day that followed was a joy: music, jokes and laughter in abundance and the most inspirational thoughts and ideas I had heard in a long time. I noticed, in particular, that whenever Burt was asked a question or started one of his explanations of the principles of the Course, he would stop, close his eyes for about a minute, and then say thank you. I asked him what this was all about and he said, 'I am consulting my Inner Teacher, the Holy Spirit.' It was then that I realised that my next teacher had to be the 'One' i.e. the one within me rather than another person or figure. I knew that what Burt had was what I was looking for and now needed to learn how to find it within myself.

At the end of our weekend of teachings from Burt, I asked him if he would continue with some follow up teachings. He answered that he and Nonnie were returning to Sweet Home in Oregon after the next day. He handed me the three Course books and said, 'Nick, you are to teach it. It is the way you will learn it.' The rest of the group were incredibly supportive of the idea that I should teach it and so I agreed to study the Course for three months, then we would start to study it together.

The very next day I began the workbook and practised the lessons on my own as best I could. It was like learning a new language and as much as I could just about remember the ideas for the day, I had no real comprehension of what they were really saying. Through the practice, I was getting to know the style of the writing and gaining a feeling for the communication itself. Even at the very beginning, it had a ring of familiarity and part of my mind knew that it was the truth.

After the three months that I had set aside for my studies, the Science of Mind and Unity groups asked me to do a series of talks on the Course over four Tuesday evenings in July. At that time, I was a regular Sunday morning speaker and operated with trigger notes to keep me 'on track'. Before the first talk I was to do, I seemed to have great difficulty in making any notes. I had no idea how to talk about what the Course was saying. I just did not know where to start.

In the afternoon prior to the first evening talk, I decided to sit and make some notes and take some quotes from the Course as a preparation. Extraordinarily and quite out of character, as I sat reading the text, I fell asleep. I slept for about two hours and had in fact only written a few words about 'Trust' which I had read from the Teachers' Manual. At seven o'clock that evening, as I stood to talk, I was prepared to say that I knew nothing about the Course and would be happy to talk about something else instead. Much to my surprise however, after the atunement prayer, I spoke easily for about an hour and answered questions about the Course with a clarity that I did not know I had.

I later listened to the tape of the talk and thought 'Where did that come from?' I had experienced the promise of the Miracle Worker's prayer on page twenty eight of the text:

'I do not have to worry about what to say or what to do,

For He Who sent me will direct me'.

The same pattern followed for the next three talks and pretty much, since that time, I make very little preparation in terms of notes, preferring to allow the inspiration to come 'in the moment'. Initially this produced nerves that I had to overcome. In time however, I have come to enjoy the feeling of being in the 'now' without thinking what I am going to say next. It is exciting to listen to what is being said by me in the flow of communication that I am receiving moment by moment.

After the fourth talk about twenty members of the group agreed they would like to study the workbook, so the following September we met to begin on lesson one. In the years of studying Science of Mind, the classes I had attended very much followed the pattern of the academic year, having an Autumn, Spring and Summer term. It felt completely right therefore, to start our year of study in the September.

In the beginning some of the group did not have the workbook so I wrote out the titles of the seven lessons to be practised over the following seven days. During the meeting I read through the instructions and discussed the key ideas that were contained within the lessons. At the start of each meeting that followed, we would report on our experiences and share in the miracles that the members of the group had experienced during the week. It was both exciting and challenging and led to many lively debates! I can with certainty say that I was stretched mentally to keep encouraging the group to continue with the lessons. There was an intensity about the teaching. I would enjoy a real high as I saw the 'lights turning on' in the minds of the group members but then there also appeared to be great resistance to the teachings making me wonder why I was doing this teaching at all. I have to say, that first year, was the most up and down year mentally and emotionally that I have ever experienced. Without the fact that I had agreed to facilitate the groups, I do not know if I would have completed the lessons, but I did get through it. Twelve of the original twenty made it through to the last lessons and my dear friend Angus, who faithfully supported me every week, confessed that he had never got past the idea of lesson one: Nothing I see means anything. He had stayed because he could see that I needed his support and love and he had faith in me. I realised then that the group was for my learning and that imparting teachings to others was only one part of the story. The more I gave away the ideas in the Course, the more those ideas strengthened my connection with the indwelling Spirit that is the source of those ideas.

On completion of the workbook for the first time in September 1985, I went through a time of great questioning with regard to all the values that I had previously held about the world, particularly those related to work, purpose and relationships. I realised that my previous investments in time and effort to achieve the usual worldly success, seemed pointless and valueless. This process that I appeared to be going through is explained in the teachers' manual in 'The Development of Trust' on page ten. I found that a lot of fear was raised in me with regard to the thought of leaving my thriving business and also my long term relationship, which was very much tied up with my business life and previous worldly living and goals. This led to a period of intense internal conflict where it seemed that the voice of worldly reason (the ego) started to present every argument as to why it would be insane to concentrate on purely teaching 'A Course in Miracles' as a life purpose. I remember one particular night, at the end of November that year, when the conflict reached its zenith. The ego threw everything at me in my mind and very gently I heard the response of the indwelling Spirit to each of the ego's fear inducing arguments. Finally the ego was silenced by my acceptance of the power of the loving thoughts flowing into my mind from the Holy Spirit. I fell into a deep and peaceful sleep. The next morning I awoke with a clarity and joy that I had never felt before. At that time in my life I always started the day with a jog for a couple of miles and on that particular morning I felt that if I had spread my arms wide I would have taken off and flown. Born within me was a feeling of being in love but without a special object for that love. I loved everyone and everything equally. My communications were clear and unequivocal and I felt a power in action that I had never known before. Two months later I had sold my shares in my business, my house was up for sale and I had bought a new home near the centre of Bournemouth where I started to teach and offer a counselling service. People arrived at my door by seeming magic and I received cash donations that met my immediate needs. I remember that in the groups I would leave a plate for donations and when I collected the money after everyone had left I felt enormous appreciation for the notes and coins I had received. I thought of this as Miracle money coming from the love of truth that is within the students.

For six months the transition continued from my previous worldly employment to what I call 'God employment'. During this time I became aware that I had not read the text of the Course all the way through. I felt inspired to put the whole of the text onto audio tape. I had the idea that if I read it aloud with the awareness that others would listen to it, then I would have to read it with consciousness and understanding. Having made this decision, as if on cue, a friend said that she could rent me her cottage in Palma, Mallorca so that I might be able to read and record the text without distraction.

On 8am on October 1ˢᵗ 1986, I drove off the ferry in Palma de Mallorca with a few possessions, my books and my Grundig tape recorder, ready to immerse myself in the text. I had no idea that those few months would in fact turn into nearly four years during which I set up two groups studying the Course, had a successful counselling practice, the most amazing adventures working for a travel company and met my wife to be, Anne.

During my time on the island, I experienced many miracles, too numerous to mention in this short introduction. I can only say that those four years were a time of grounding the principles of 'The Course' into my being through constant demand of practice.

In 1990, Anne and I returned to the U.K. with the intention of founding a 'Centre for Inner Peace.' We were open to the idea of finding a property somewhere between Malvern in Worcestershire, England, where my parents lived, and Inverness, Scotland, the home of Anne's family. In the meantime, I was invited to teach 'The Course' by Gloria and John Houghton at their 'Guiding Light Centre' in Malvern.

In September 1991, Anne and I married in Scotland in one of the most beautiful places I have seen, The Great Glen just north of Inverness. With hindsight I can so clearly see an unfolding story that now seems like the pieces of a jigsaw puzzle fitting into place. On New Year's Day in 1992, over a celebration lunch, my parents suddenly declared that they had an idea that Anne and I could combine with them to buy a place that would be suitable for us to have a 'Teaching Centre', and for them to have some land for growing vegetables and a bigger garden: a final home for them to retire to.

A short time later my mother found somewhere for us to look at. It was just outside Worcester, near a village called Kempsey, with great access around the country via the nearby M5 motorway. There was a large red brick farmhouse, converted with its original stables into two homes. It had a barn, converted for social/domestic use, perfect for a larger teaching room, and also a car park and nearly nine acres of land. It was perfect and just as Anne and I had visualised whilst living in Mallorca. It became our home and 'Centre' and is where we still live and teach.

In September 1992 we started our teaching here and immediately people arrived as if on cue just as described in the Teachers' manual:

'Certain pupils have been assigned to each of God's teachers and they begin to look for him as soon as he has answered the call'

It is now over twenty years later, and we have had literally thousands of teaching and learning groups here at our home and we have hosted many other teachers from around the UK and the USA. I have also enjoyed thousands of one to one healing and counselling sessions where I have learned to listen both internally and externally. We have made a huge number of friends who have become our extended family, all studying the Course.

Without a doubt, listening is the key to connectedness with the Holy Spirit. It is the way to make the link with that internal Oneness with Love that then communicates through our own consciousness. With practice, the connection becomes as easy as making a call on a mobile phone. Prayer is the activation of the link and miracles, which are communications of Love, flow through into expression.

Whenever I am writing and in the flow of communication, I feel a great sense of peace and well- being. This is the constant message of the Holy Spirit i.e. regardless of what is going on in the outer world, reported from one body to another, there is nothing to fear. Love is the only and absolute reality. Truly all is well for now and forever.

Over the past twenty years I have made it my practice to link with the Holy Spirit prior to all my groups, seminars, public talks and one to one sessions. Sometimes I will ask a specific question to allow the miracle I am to give to be received in my mind and a selection of these communications are included in the third section this book. Throughout my time with the course I have received constant invitation and encouragement from the Holy Spirit to understand the ideas of the Course more fully. It is my loving pleasure to now share that invitation with you.

Nick Davis

Part II

Peace Be unto Thee, Stranger

Peace be unto thee, stranger, enter and be not afraid.
I have left the gate open and thou art welcome in my home.
There is room in my house for all.
I have swept the hearth and lighted the fire.
The room is warm and cheerful and you will find comfort and rest
within.
The table is laid and the fruits of Life are spread before thee.
The wine is here also, it sparkles in the light.
I have set a chair for you where the sunbeams dance through the
shade.
Sit and rest and refresh your soul.
Eat of the fruit and drink the wine.
All, all is yours, and you are welcome.

Ernest Holmes ~ The Science of Mind (Introduction)

Chapter One:
From a Loving Brother...

You are going to have a revelation. It is going to be revealed to you that you are not a body with all its limitations but that you are in fact invulnerable and eternal. You will see that you are not subject to change or harm and that your nature is purely loving.

In the liberation that occurs with revelation, you will know that there is nothing to fear because you cannot be harmed by anything or anyone in the world. You will have returned for a period of time to who and what you really are and it will be such a transforming experience, that you will never return to your former perception of yourself. The peace that this experience will bring is beyond words and literally passes all understanding. It therefore cannot be communicated to another so that they can experience it. It can lead them to their own revelation if they open their minds to it through miracles.

I am inviting you to open yourself to having a revelation and although this is guaranteed to you in time, there is a way to shorten that time to experiencing it. You can shorten the time immeasurably, indeed by thousands of years, through miracles. Miracles undo all the defences that you have in your mind to the truth of who and what you are, which may I remind you, is perfection itself. But perhaps I had best explain to you what has happened to you and why you do not seem to be experiencing your invulnerability and perfection...

A long time ago in time but only an instant ago in eternity, you contemplated a very amusing thought. You imagined that you could be separate or different from your Creator! You actually could not achieve this, as you remain an idea in the Mind of your Creator forever, but as a being of free will to choose whatever you want to think, you could certainly have a go at imagining it ...and so you did. This did not produce a change in you at all but because your thoughts have power, you were able to produce a very realistic world in which this separation with its differences could be seen to be accomplished. You also seem to have produced an instrument called a body through which you could perceive this world and be convinced about it.

You then forgot about the truth and though the devastation of the experience of apartness from your Creator was felt i.e. a terrible state of fear, you tried to learn to live with it. This fear has never left you although you have tried to distract yourself with all the magical inventions you have produced with your imagination. This fear never leaves you but it can seem to be denied and ignored very effectively at times. Because the fear is in your mind however, and your thoughts are powerful, it manifests in frightening events like diseases, disasters and death, which all seem to reinforce the separation and vulnerability. It appears that you are then a victim of these things rather than the maker. In this way of seeing, it appears that you are powerless and that there is a power outside of you seeking your demise and final annihilation.

When you realise that you are the maker or rather mis-creator of fear, then you will enter into a programme of undoing the fears you have made up in your mind. This process is called the Atonement i.e. the returning to at-one-ment and it is the real purpose of time. Time is available for you to unlearn the false beliefs that originate from the thought of separation. Each person will find their way back to Truth in time but there is a curriculum available which can lead you directly through the process of

Atonement; it is called 'A Course In Miracles'. This course is the most effective course that has ever been produced to release you from your suffering.

It may at this stage seem difficult to accept that all your problems stem from seeing wrongly, but seeing wrongly is the one and only problem. You need a correction of sight, and a miracle is that correction. A miracle enables you to see everything the way it is, rather than the way you perceive it. Before you can start on the healing of your perception, it is necessary for you to realise that you **are** seeing wrongly. A change of heart is therefore required, whereby you are willing to be taught by a teacher who can lead you out of the maze of misperceptions that have trapped you in the world of illusions.

This willingness has to come from **you** and cannot be forced upon you. You have free will and that will is total. It has to be said however that discomfort in the world of separation cannot be endured forever, so at some stage, you will hear your own call for help acknowledged, and in that call lies the seed of the answer. Your inner being will verbalise 'there must be a better way' and the answer will follow.

Once you have acknowledged your desire for help, you will see that help has always been there and that the world, viewed correctly, is an answer to the problem of separation. It is a single shift that changes everything you see, and you will know that you have been answered since the beginning of time but were psychologically blind and deaf to the solution. What is entailed in this single shift? You must want it and want it truly!

It is said in the bible that the rich man was willing to sell all that he had, to purchase the pearl of great price. Let me immediately reassure you that this does not refer to monetary wealth, but that he was willing to give up his cherished beliefs about himself and the world. He was willing to be corrected because he knew his attitudes and purposes were erroneous. In some ways this is harder to give up than all the material possessions you own. The acceptance of being wrong is seen as a loss of face: your image in your own sight and others is about to be lost and because you made up this image, you value it like one of your own creations. But fear not, for when you see the pain of maintaining an image instead of being who you really are, you will be happy to give it up. In the giving up there is no sacrifice; there is in fact joy in you and throughout the whole kingdom. This is what was meant when it was said that 'greater love hath no man that he lay down his life for his brother.' You cannot literally lay down your life because life is eternal, but you can lay down your image and the temporary life in time and space of that image. To do so is the greatest gift you can make in this world to yourself, your brothers and your sisters.

So this is my invitation to you, to come with me on the greatest journey of your life, the journey into your own consciousness. You will see such wonders in the changes in your thoughts that you will know they are miracles. There will be no limit to their effects upon the way you see, and their influence on how others will see. This adventure is a journey and you will gather friends, both visible and invisible. These friends will walk with you and there will be healing, celebrations and much joy. The only regret will be not having seen the journey sooner, but that will be swallowed up by the realisation that time, especially the past, is meaningless and imagined.

The adventure is 'picking up your bed and walking', for you have been stuck in your bed asleep for many a long lifetime. As you start to walk on your journey, the strength will return to your system and you will be a man or woman of activity and presence. You will be a leader and teacher amongst others, but always a disciple and student of Love itself, for this is the return to Love and it is the greatest adventure of all. Through this adventure it will be revealed that who you truly are is what you have been seeking all along.

Mind is the Master power that moulds and makes,
And Man is Mind, and evermore he takes
The tool of Thought, and, shaping what he wills,
Brings forth a thousand joys, a thousand ills:-
He thinks in secret, and it comes to pass:
Environment is but his looking-glass.

James Allen ~As a Man Thinketh

Chapter Two
Illusions and Miracles

Before you can understand miracles you must first understand what an illusion is, for a miracle undoes an illusion so that you may see the truth.

The first illusion that must be undone is that miracles are amazing physical happenings. Radical changes in world events, manipulation of matter or incredible healings in the body are not the miracles I speak of. Outward changes may well appear to happen as a result of miracles, but the miracle itself occurs at the level of mind. Illusions also occur at the level of mind and could be described as thinking that something is happening in a certain way, when in fact it isn't. Thoughts can be out of accord with facts and produce distortions like trying to make facts 'fit in' with theories.

Theorising or analysing and explaining appearances are where most of your mental energies are expended and in themselves produce illusions. You spend hours trying to explain the inexplicable. An illusionist will have you trying to work out how he took a white rabbit out of a hat or made a dove out of a handkerchief, but it is simply a trick of the eye. All illusions are deceptions and rely upon your mind being tricked into believing them. This is what is meant by 'judge not by appearances'. Appearances/illusions are made to deceive and their purpose is to make you believe that something is happening when it is not.

Miracles will take the 'scales from your eyes' and you will see what is truly present. You will realise that what is there is good – very good! So in a way a miracle does not do anything, it merely undoes a false perception and reveals what is already there.

The result of miracles is healing. Health is the natural state that is uncovered when the illusion that hid it is undone. Sickness is of the mind when it is filled with illusions. A sick mind is one full of illusions; a healthy mind is one where miracles have replaced illusions and restored the mind to sanity.

A sick mind sees a sick world and a sick body and seeks to correct it, not by healing the mind, but by trying to alter the 'appearances'. It is a bit like looking into a mirror and noticing on the image a blemish, which you then try to rub away on the mirror with a cloth, by using a chemical or by covering it up with a plaster. Trying to fix appearances that are the results of the illusions of the mind is called magic. It sometimes appears to work because the mind believes that if it can't see something in form, it has been healed, but that is another trick. A hypnotic suggestion can make a person believe he is a dog and act like a dog, but it is just a suggestion and it will wear off because the mind cannot be shackled by untruth. Suggestions need to be reinforced again and again because the underlying thought, the underlying truth is still there i.e. the Thought of God which is what you truly are.

A miracle does not change the truth; it undoes a lie and thus brings the mind back into alignment with the truth. When the mind is in perfect alignment, there is harmony and peace. The conflict is one between lies and truth: truth does not make the conflict, but lies make an imagined conflict whilst the mind believes in them. Once again we are dealing with illusions and all illusions are imagined and have no reality: that is why they are called illusions. Illusions being unreal are therefore subject to change and they will take away their effects with them as they are dissolved by miracles. It seems therefore as if the miracle has made something disappear when it was in fact, the illusion disappearing into the nothingness from whence it came.

All sickness in the world is the manifestation of illusions. We may say that illusions in the mind produce sickness and in doing so we are correctly stating that only the mind can be sick. To be more accurate still, only thoughts held by the mind can be sick and as these 'sick' thoughts are released, so too is the mind released.

The underlying thought that is behind all illusions is that you can do harm and be harmed. The two go together but were started with the thought that you can harm. As has already been said you were created invulnerable by an invulnerable Creator, but somehow you imagined you could change Creation and therefore could change your Self. This, of course, is the birth of vulnerability and fear from which you have been trying to escape ever since. You cannot heal this by trying to make yourself safe by physical means. I am sure you can see that by doing so you are retaining the fear and endeavouring to live with it by defending yourself from its effects.

This is where 'magic' comes in to seemingly save you from fear. You have sought many magical solutions to healing the effects of fear but have not seen the insanity of the thought that gave rise to fear in the first place. You cannot harm or be harmed and therefore have no need to protect your Self. All defences are therefore self attack and consequently lead to disastrous effects in the dream world e.g. experiences of attacking and being attacked by an insurmountable enemy with the odds stacked against you.

Now perhaps you can see a little more of what the world is, how it is made up and how only miracles which undo the illusion can free you from your self- made world.

To summarise:

- You arc as God created you, invulnerable and eternal. If you experience fear you have made up the illusion that you can harm God and Your Self.
- The miracle undoes this illusion and restores you to the truth that you **are** invulnerable and eternal.

The illusion need only be seen to lose all power over you, just as when you have discovered the illusionist's trick of pulling the rabbit out of the hat, you then cease to be interested.

When you know that you cannot harm or be harmed, what is the point of playing the game any more? Nobody is impressed for very long by something that clearly doesn't work and does not do anything. The desire to be creative re-awakens and you move on to that which is truly satisfying and brings real joy.

Whilst you believe in the separation from God, you will seek magical solutions as to why you are feeling so unhappy. You will ask the question again and again and the ego will answer again and again with many answers, all with the same fundamental ingredients:

- You will be told you are missing something, but never the truth.
- You will be told that you are lacking in yourself and need to fulfil yourself by doing something, becoming something or gaining something. However, when you attain by doing, becoming or gaining something, the feeling of lack remains and you will soon ask the question again.

Magical solutions all revolve around never questioning the validity of the separation. If only you would look at separation, you would see that it is quite impossible to be apart from your Source and remain a conscious thinking being. If it were the case that you were separate from your Source, your life would have ended and you would no longer exist… but you are still alive and thinking, thereby proving the non-existence of separation.

So what is separation? It is entirely a thought; a false thought in the mind of the thinker, but as all thoughts appear as images in your mind, it produces a state that does not exist except in your imagination. First there is the imagined effect and then a cure is sought to fix the effect. The world is filled with solutions to a problem that does not exist. Is it not a rather subtle thought that enters into the mind of that which is perfect to suggest that it is not perfect and thereby should seek out what is wrong with it? This is what has happened in your mind i.e. you have believed that you are imperfect or lacking and that you need to find out what is missing. But you are not imperfect, nor lacking. Therefore, are you seeking for something that does not exist i.e. an illusion?

Cease your seeking, see the error and simply correct it by accepting the answer that has been given to me by my Creator for you. A miracle is the answer and all you have to do is to invite it, in any moment. Know that what you perceive is untrue and ask for the correction. You do not have to provide the correction; it is already there, but you must let go of what you are holding in your mind that hides it.

What is the error? It is some sort of judgement or blame against someone or something that keeps the mind projecting an image to cover what is truly there to see. Your perceptions are projected outwards making images that then appear real to you. You must learn to doubt the images you see and accept the truth of what I am telling you instead. The world is a deception, an illusion that appears and convinces you that there is something there. It is a constant appearance of danger, peopled by figures with happenings and events that you are a victim of, unless you learn to protect and defend yourself effectively. Have you not noticed how much   revolves around self-defence and how much effort is put to planning for your protection?

All that is being asked of you is to be willing to question, to release some painful thoughts and then see what appears. The only cost to you is the giving up of pain and suffering of every kind. There will be no more sacrifices on your part and no more compromises, only a complete receiving of everything that is good, lovely and truly satisfying.

Why are you still hesitant? Is it because you think you are not worthy? Let me tell you once and for all, you are a perfect child of God created in the image and likeness of Infinite Love Itself, and because of that, the Kingdom is yours. Do not doubt me but also do not lose your reason. Just ask your self: Is it reasonable that an all powerful loving presence would make a mistake and create a being that could lose the perfection given to it? You are dreaming, wake up and see the truth and remember. Your magical solutions have failed since the beginning of time. You cannot fix what is not broken and to keep endeavouring to do so is insane. Stop asking what is wrong with you and ask to see the truth about you. You have been calling for an answer: the answer is here and it is a miracle. Accept and join the Atonement and learn that you have never left Heaven and that all is truly well.

Let me recognize the problem so it can be solved.

ACIM workbook ~ lesson 79.

Chapter Three:
Seeing the Problem

You may well ask what is time for? It is a question that needs to be answered so that you may use it effectively. Time is the space in which you make up your mind to choose again. Time began in the instant you thought of separating from your Creator and will end when the thought ceases to be focussed on with your mind. Time itself is neutral and in a sense has no meaning. However, it can be used or abused according to the purpose it is put to. In time you can be paralysed by indecision for what appears to be many eons, but your 'will' cannot be held back forever. There comes a point when the decision to see the truth again is made, or maybe it is better explained as the decision to undo the false is made.

Time is painful to the mind held in indecision, but to the one who has chosen again it is kind and a happy dream of awakening takes place as a gentle grace. Hanging on to illusions takes great effort and a deep tiredness is felt by you who have held on to them for so long.

But what are illusions? They are nothing. When they are gone it is realised that they never existed and the past in all its longevity is dispelled in an instant. What in truth can delay what is forever present and always known? When the dawn arrives in all its magnificence, the long dark night is forgotten and never thought of again.

Time then is a blessing to you, for it is a gift from your Creator to let you choose to awaken gently. You will not be confused by the sudden shock of the difference between Reality and the world of thought that you have been seeing. An instantaneous shift from total darkness into light, however beautiful and magnificent that light may be, may confuse your mind. So it is that a gentle passage in time and space is planned for you. All the figures in your dream are used to let the dawn be a harmonious melody and to bring you out of your sleep in peace and comfort.

When you do see the light it will be awe-inspiringly beautiful and you will be lost for words. This is because your Creator has created such perfection that it is literally unbelievable and therefore can only be known by your perfect mind. This may give you an insight i.e. that you are capable of experiencing perfection. What a phenomenal kind of 'Being' you are to be able to know perfection. This realisation can instantly dissolve all self-doubt and in fact **will** instantly dissolve all self-doubt, which is where the initial error occurred: a moment of self-doubt, and you have been self doubting ever since.

To reassure you is the task I have been given and the one that you will take up and give to all the others who have entered into the same self-doubt. To reassure is to affirm again and affirming is but to state the truth about your Self. You could not, and have not, changed your Self and so remain as you were created in all perfection. When you once again see the light, you will see only this and know that what you saw only a moment before was an illusion and nothing more. A moment later and even that realisation will have gone and you will once again be seeing your Self as if that seeing had never been interrupted.

You may ask in your present vision why such a little thought, such a tiny mistake can produce so much of a world. At one time you may have looked in a distorting mirror; only a slight adjustment to the shape in the mirror can change everything that is seen in it. This world is a mirror that reflects a tiny adjustment and consequently everything that is seen is distorted accordingly.

Your mind needs straightening out and the appearances naturally change with it. You need some straight talking and some clear listening. Miracles are the straight talking that correct the adjustment made to your mind when you contemplated the impossible thought of separation. Each miracle comes from the thought that says, you cannot change the Works of the Creator including your Self - see this and be free.

You can give this miracle as you have received it from me. This makes us equals. As miracle-givers we are all equals. When your thinking is aligned or straightened by miracles, you will be thinking like me and that is true connectedness and closeness. You have heard of people living together and starting to think alike. When you and I think alike, we will be living together in true closeness, and this is at-one-ment.

Your mind will become miracle minded like mine and eventually this will be achieved by all. The illusory split in the mind caused by a distorting thought will be healed and all appearances of distortion will disappear enabling your reflection to return to normal and you will be at peace. You will not be frightened by what you see: in fact, you will love and praise your Creator again for what perfection He has made.

Sometimes it is said in the explanation of 'magic' that 'it is all done with mirrors'. This is how the famous disappearing trick on the stage is done. So it is that true creation has disappeared by a trick of mirrors. Your physical eye is a mirror that receives light from outside and the images are then judged by the mind in relation to its past learning to say what they are. All the images are in the eye and experienced there. Yet to your mind, you would say that the images were 'out there' and away in the distance in some cases! This is a trick and gives us an insight to one of the illusions that needs healing. Everything you see is in the mind and only there can correction take place. If you were looking in a mirror and saw a pimple on your face, would you heal it by trying to cover it up on the mirror with a plaster or some ointment? The moment you moved, it would re-appear in another place in the mirror. This is what material healing tries to do i.e. to change appearances using physical means applied to images. With every attempt to do so, we have a side effect - we see the pimple again from another angle or in another place. To bring what is seen outside back into the mind enables true healing to take place. Only the mind can make a mistake therefore, only the mind needs correction. The correction is a miracle.

When the mistake was first made it was naked or uncovered, but because guilt came into the mind with the mistake, Adam and Eve are said to have covered themselves with a fig leaf. The error was effectively hidden from them. In doing this it was unable to be healed. Recognising the error is the first step to healing, for once seen it can be undone or forgiven. As our Creator never condemned Adam and Eve, the guilt existed only in their feverish imagination, and so it remained unforgiven by their minds. The love from the Creator never changed but the feverish dream in Adam and Eve was followed with thoughts of 'sin and punishment'. The world was the picture of sin and punishment being acted out by bodies over and over again, until the Light came into the world, and with it the beginning of the end of the world of sin and punishment. For the Light demonstrated there was no sin and no punishment in the Mind of the Creator – only in the minds of those who saw themselves as bodies and were therefore blind to the Light.

The Great Awakening began with the return of the Christ Light and has continued ever since. Now it is time for you. All that is needed is for you to wake up and see. There is no long journey, no fight against sin, no time consuming practices to break free from the body; just Christ's Vision, a gift willingly given to a willing and open mind.

God's gifts are given unto all of us impersonally and wholly without favouritism; there is no provision in the kingdom of God for leaving anyone outside of his Love and Grace.

Joel S. Goldsmith ~ The Gift of Love

Chapter Four:
Choosing the Gift of Heaven

Be still and listen! Hear my Voice and know that I am speaking to you the Holy One: The loving child of an infinitely loving parent. You have never changed except in the momentary dream that passed a long time ago but left a bitter aftertaste that has confused you. Let the confusion cease in the simplicity of my words. You are as you were created and no sin has come to alter you or make a mockery of the Original Creation. I invite you again to pick up the Workbook that has been written for you and make its lessons your learning goal for your time experience. There is no better use of time and I mean that unequivocally. The world of sin and punishment is meaningless. Why would you spend another instant in it when you can have the world of miracles I have made for you?

Each lesson IS a miracle; each lesson carries the joyous message of forgiveness and release to you and all the Children of the Creator. This is the new world I promised you. The other one was made a long time ago and has not yet been fully unchosen. Choose again - the only choice you can now make is Heaven. Just because your last choice was a faulty one does not mean your next one will be. There is only the choice of Heaven or nothing, and nothing is no choice at all! Join me in my choice and listen as I tell you of all the wonders you will see: the old world will be transformed in the twinkling of an eye and you will never doubt again. I have a gift for you.   Just give me an instant of your time and it will be yours.

The love you will feel is inexpressible; the peace so absorbing that you can never think of anything else. The joy is so elevating that there is no possibility of your mind being tempted into sadness again. This Realm of Ideas that was yours in the beginning will be fully remembered and it will be as if you had never forgotten it. Everyone in their Reality will be with you. There will be no loss but more to gain than you can ever imagine.

The only reason that you do not accept it now is that the thought of sacrifice has entered your mind and disturbed your thinking. You think giving up the world you now see is a sacrifice, instead of realising that by seeing this false world, you have sacrificed Reality in all its glory. There is no sacrifice in truth, only an illusion of sacrifice. You could never give up what the Creator has given you, but you can lose sight of it by concentrating on another world of thought.

How simple it is: you are given everything in return for nothing, but you must see first that it is nothing that you are seeing. That is why I invite you again to do the lessons of the Workbook of A Course In Miracles, for if you do, they will lead you very quickly to the realisation of the seeing of nothing and it will only be a moment before you choose again to ask for the gift of everything.

I say again because, by your own free will you chose in the gift of your creation the gift of everything...and it was given. You could never lose it, only lose sight of it. That is why the only healing, the only miracle, is to return your sight to you. You have been covering your eyes and imagining all sorts of strange things. Remove your hand from your eyes and place it in mine as we were created and all will be restored as your eyes become accustomed to the Light.

It has been said 'Ask and it shall be given'. This does not refer to the things you think you need in the world, but that which you require to return to your mind the awareness of another world. In this other world there are no needs and the only prayer is one of gratitude for what has already been given. You need only to ask for the Truth, without your deciding already what it is, then it is given to you, or rather, it is returned to your awareness.

Why should you ask for what you already have in Truth? You ask because you rejected it and accepted an alternative. The alternative was 'nothing' and you have made do with 'nothing' ever since, but you must see it is nothing before you will release it. Vision will give you this i.e. the Vision that comes with the Light. I am the Light that gives you the Vision to see this so that you may simply choose again. I am motivating you to give up your miscreations so that the whole of Creation in all its Glory may be given back to your recognition. To recognise is to know again as you knew before. In the beginning you knew the Kingdom of Heaven and you will know it again because truly It is the only Reality you can know. The other state can only be invented and perceived by a mind that thinks it is separate and what is that but imagination.

No matter how far you have gone in the teaching of duality, no matter what a mess of things you have made, it is all cast away the moment you become one with this glorious true self called the Christ.

Walter C Lanyon ~ The Eyes of the Blind.

Chapter Five:
The Return to Knowledge

Once again you may ask how you return to Knowledge. The way is simple: you exchange each illusion for a miracle; your point of view for my point of view. What is your resistance to that? You may say, 'I value my point of view'; 'I am entitled to my point of view'. In the world people fight over points of view, they argue and defend sometimes unto death. The task is simple, the resistance more complex. First your mind needs straightening out so that you can see that what you value is indeed the source of your pain. When you see that your will is to be happy, you will automatically choose to ditch the source of pain.

You may say that it would take a miracle to see that something so valued by the world is required to be given up before the return of Knowledge. Indeed that is what it is - a miracle. I saw it, and my mind is part of yours so, part of you has already chosen it. Now it is only a matter of time before the rest of your mind catches up (so to speak). There is no going back, only a steady going forward by letting go of the illusions of the past. Your own point of view could never be true because you are not on your own. As you listen to me and hear my voice in your mind, it becomes so obvious that the realisation occurs that 'an own point of view' is ridiculous, even funny and can be gently laughed away.

Lightness of approach is always the way of miracles because there is no substance to illusions: they are blown away by the gentle Breath of God. So are you ready to work with miracles? Remember I am in your mind and I am ready. The more you realise that you are not alone, by listening to me, the more we can accomplish together. I need your co-operation because the whole of creation is a co-operation and so is the Atonement i.e. the undoing of the thought of separation.

Working miracles comes first from the desire to not accept error in yourself and thereby in those you see who are part of yourself. This desire will grow into action. It is when you wish to activate the undoing process that opportunities to perform miracles will be presented by your brothers and sisters. You will see your errors in them and if they are willing you can join in undoing them together. This joining is the greatest of joys in the world because it is an acknowledgement of oneness, and oneness is Truth and Love. See how your brothers and your sisters are your saviours by giving you the opportunity to know your Self again.

You are joy and you are love and knowing your Self is experiencing love and joy. That is why it was said, 'Man know thyself' because you contain everything that you are looking for. What you have been looking for is what you have been looking with. You have been searching for your Self without asking who it is that is searching. You are the one you have always been looking for. You have projected parts of yourself onto all the 'so called' others that walk the world with you. As they rejoin with you, you remember. The miracle restores your memory and you recognise who you are again. The Creation is who you are, and how beautiful and perfect it is.

These opportunities to join in miracles will be given to you; each opportunity a healing encounter, and both of you will be a little nearer the revelation of who you are. This is the plan and I am in charge of this plan, bringing you together at the right moment. All you need do is listen to my voice, agree to the undoing of your misperception, and accept the correction in your mind. The more you do, the more convinced you will be and you will become more miracle-minded. That is to say, your mind will be more like mine: my mind is already free of illusions and soon yours will be too. Miracles will then be automatic and require no effort on your part at all. This is potential in you and in all the Children of God. It is good to acknowledge it now so that you realise it is only a matter of time and not open to question. The Atonement is guaranteed in time. It is the only event that is fully guaranteed because it is Eternal and therefore Real.

Meanwhile there is much to do and I am calling upon you to do it. This is my invitation: I invite you to become a miracle worker which is your natural profession. In this, you will join the Brotherhood i.e. those who have awakened and become glad. Fulfil your destiny in time so that you may return to Eternity which is true Knowledge. In doing so, you enable your brothers and sisters to do the same. The acceptance of the Atonement is your first and your last responsibility, for in that act of acceptance you have fulfilled your part in the Great Plan of freedom for the Son of God. So accept, be glad, and be thankful that it is as simple as that. What else would God's Answer be but simplicity itself?

Your way *then* will be one continuous round of blessing.
Wherever you go will My Light shine and My Love radiate forth
about you creating Peace, Concord, Unity.

Joseph S. Benner ~The Impersonal Life.

Chapter Six:
The Healing Agreement

Healing is an agreement made by two people that their minds may be healed. To ask for healing is to invite your own true thoughts to be your own again. To be sick is to be fooled into thinking that the illusions of the ego are real. The sickness grips the mind by presenting evidence of sickness to the bodily senses which then report back to the mind that indeed there is reality to the sickness. You may ask how you can free yourself from such convincing witnesses. When you are in the cycle of such an attack you need my help to break the spell. To do this you need to ask me to think for you. If you turn to your own thinking the ego will offer only magic: a spell to bind you more tightly to illusions. This is the true meaning of spellbound: your mind is gripped by appearances that captivate your imagination and spiral you down into hopelessness and consequently sleep. You cannot die but you can dream of dying, again and again, until you see that it is not a solution but simply a paralysis of will.

At any time, in any instant, you can ask me for healing, in the understanding that it means to join me in my thinking; thereby giving up yours. This is the true meaning of release: releasing your mind and its thinking to me. You believe this may imprison your will, but your will will be returned to you and you will see that the ego had made a hostage of you through trickery and deception. When your will is returned to you, it is only a matter of a short time until your freedom is complete. For now, let me do your thinking for you. Do not be insulted by this, for I am only giving your own thoughts back to you. They have been kept safe whilst you have been enthralled by the world. You are coming back to your Self: you have not been your Self for a while, or at least, you have not been aware of your Self for a while!

When you ask for healing, you are taking responsibility for your miscreations of sickness, admitting that your mind has been listening to the ego but that you no longer wish to do so. You are saying:

"I would listen to you and open my mind to you. I would join my mind to yours and let true Cause and Effect be my experience."

True cause is Perfect Love and its effect is wholeness and perfection. Healing is accomplished by returning your mind to true causation: Perfect God, Perfect Son, Perfect Being.

The Atonement was made for you, a loving gift from your Loving Creator to free you from your own miscreations: what you made with your mind whilst you were trying to think apart from the One mind. It is a gift that frees you from all suffering and pain. You made suffering and pain as a form of self-punishment in the false idea that this, in some way, would free you from the guilt induced by the ego for your harmless and innocent contemplation of the daft thought of separation.

The Atonement brings you back to this 'thought of separation', so that you can see it in the light and gently laugh it away in the soft humour that forgiveness has blessed you with. The smile of your own forgiveness then extends to all your brothers and sisters and they are freed from the thought of separation themselves.

The whole world is a product of this one thought: 'separation'. Is it not amazing to see what a thought can produce? When you see this, you will also see what a single thought can undo. That is the miracle: a single thought that can undo a whole 'world'. Now you see why there is no order of difficulty in miracles.

A loving thought can have no limitations placed upon it. A fear thought produces nothing but a dreamscape: a smokescreen attempting to hide an eternal and glorious Reality. Blow lightly upon the rings of smoke and you will see them disappear into nothingness. There is more joy in this than making shapes of dust and attempting to gain impossible pleasures from them. Even in this however, you can admire the ingenious mind that is capable of manufacturing so many imaginary forms of such complexity from what is but a single grain of dust. Begin to see this and you will have a tiny inkling of the creating that you will do when liberated from the thrall of a grain of dust, and the revelation of a universe which awaits your playful nature.

What will you do when this liberation from the thrall of dust takes place, you may ask. Your revelation will reveal this; a eureka moment as you have never known in this world. It will take your breath away from the dust and a new breath will fill your being: the Breath of God. Not the imaginary god of the world but the Infinite Source of All, the Mover of Life itself, the Supreme Principle behind all that is and ever shall be. The Love you will know is beyond the alphabet and all its symbolic words. If you will be ever so quiet with me just for an instant, I will breathe a little with you and you will feel what it means to be One, undivided in mind and heart where only holiness exists: peace without opposite. Thy will is restored at last.

Nick Davis

Everything becomes spiritual once the door of the chamber of the heart is open. If a man is a musician, then his music is celestial: if he is a poet, then his poetry is spiritual: if he is an artist then his art is a spiritual work; whatever he may do in life the divine spirit manifests.

Hazrat Inayat Khan ~ The Awakening of the Human Spirit.

Chapter Seven:
Learning by Reward

All true healing takes place through reward. No one learns from pain because pain is the absence of teaching. When you are learning from me, which occurs when our minds are joined, think of the rewards. Another way of saying 'by their fruits ye shall know them,' is 'Love is known by its reward.' Love is the word for the gift given by the Creator to his Creation. In this gift is everything that the Creator is. All that the Creator is, is extended to you and in that is total and absolute fulfilment. Love is its own reward.

When you join with me, remember I am the Atonement because 'the Father and I are one', and you are reconnected to Love. What pleasure is there in pain now you have learnt the difference? Now you cannot help but choose joy. It is only whilst you did not remember the difference between Love and fear that you kept trying to choose pleasurable forms of pain. Love is all; fear is nothing. Choosing different images in the emptiness is as much as you can do. To judge some as pleasurable and some as painful is a sleepy game only dreaming minds would be fooled by.

The reward of Love is everything. The effect of 'sleep' is a tiredness that leaves the mind preoccupied by images projected from a dark and hidden thought of madness. Look again, my beloved brother, and you will see right next to that hidden thought a key to treasure hidden from your gaze. Take that key and unlock the fixed opinion of sin that chains your mind to illusions. Throw open the door and invite me in, as I am inviting you. I will never force entry, as you would misunderstand and re-lock the door, hiding the key in a darker fear. I stand at the door and wait. My patience is limitless because it is made of certainty and love. As I wait, I sing a simple song learned in Heaven that you have not fully forgotten; the one the Creator sang with us in our Creation. You hear it now but not with ears, no, much deeper. It is the call for Love that rings in the very core of your being; the call to return to joy.

Notice your resistance to Love. See the cost that resistance brings. Do not ask why you resist because in truth the resistance is not yours, it is the ego's. The ego is something you have made, a thought of fear that pretends it is alive but cannot be. It is kept going by your sympathy. You joined with a thought that had no substance but you would not let it go, believing it to be real. Let it go with love or should I say, love and let it go. For when you experience the reward of Love, the ego is gone. You have learned there is no choice, but only a remembering of the true identity of Love: an awakening, a dawn that sees a dream forgotten in an instant, never to be dreamed again. Just as it is when you awaken now from your earthly slumbers and dreams are forgotten in the fullness of the day.

Learn no more from suffering. Learn from me instead and we will laugh and laugh in the celebration of a conversation we were having a moment ago. A moment briefly interrupted by a firefly which mesmerized your senses, before being extinguished in the flame of purification. What was the conversation? Was it not praise of what the Creator had provided for your birthday? Listen again fully to me and let us continue to celebrate your Creation with more delighted laughter, for you are indeed worthy of the celebration of a whole Universe.

How must you think of your brothers and sisters? You are not special; you are not different; you are awakening and they are too. I am with them all as I am with you. I made my promise and my promise was made by God through me, so that when I said 'I will never leave you comfortless', I said it for all, including you.

Each will awaken to my voice and I will lead each and every one as I am leading you. The Love is the same, only the scenery is different for each one in their dreams. See the many different scenes in which your brothers and sisters have chosen to listen to me. Some will choose tragedy, others comedies of errors but remember, they are only scenes within a larger play, written by a Mighty Author who has chosen a message of mighty power. This is a love story, a lover saving his/her beloved from a thought of temptation. In the story the beloved forgets his/her identity and the lover faithfully remains by his/her side gently reminding him/her who they are in truth.

I have given you a beloved to gently remind you too. I shall give you many beloveds for you to whisper to, on my behalf, whilst their inner listening is affected by the 'thought of temptation'.

Whisper with me my words of light and revival and feel the fellowship of the Brotherhood. What a play has been written! What a stage has been set! What a part for you - a saviour amidst saviours; each and every one the hero and the heroine; a star amongst stars. You are all the special ones because one role was made for everyone.

Take to the stage my brother to play your part and inspire the audience. Their turn will come and they will know what to do, because they learnt it by heart from you.

The Presence or the The Voice Celestial, becoming audible to all
who develop the inner ear.

Ernest S. Holmes and Fenwicke L. Holmes ~ The Voice Celestial

Chapter Eight:
The Healing Voice

Without doubt your biggest problem is dissociating from identification with the body. It is probably one of the illusions that is least questioned. It seems that in the world your starting point was being born as a body; sensing everything as a body; growing up as a body and learning more as you go, so that you base everything from the viewpoint of being physical. This leaves in place that underlying unexpressed word 'death', always behind the scenes whispering to you through the appearances of the world.

This identification with the body is how the ego is able to maintain itself. The ego cleverly promotes guilt when you start to question this identification because you no longer sympathise with the experiences of the body and start to see the invulnerability of the mind in all situations and circumstances. It will suggest to you that you no longer care, are emotionally lacking and even callous for not believing in the pains and sufferings of 'other bodies'.

This is why dissociation from the body is such a challenge for you and will manifest in your relationships as experiences of feeling attacked for learning the truth. For as others become aware that you are no longer thinking like them, it feels to them as if you are attacking their thought systems. This gives rise to attempts to defend themselves by trying to make you believe in what they are going through to 'bring you back to them.' This activity, although appearing to be happening outside of you, is a reflection of the underlying conversation that is taking place in your own mind. Old patterns of thinking try to reinforce themselves: the belief that you are a body is very long held and has millions of years of history.

The challenge of dissociating from identification with the body would appear to be overwhelming without miracles and my help. By joining with me in the one mind, you immediately free yourself from body-identification and experience the light and peace that joining brings. You then become more objective about the body when you return to your own sense i.e. you start to see it as an instrument or useful tool rather than a 'self' and you will see how others are using their body rather than 'being' their body.

The objectivity about the body would also free you from beliefs about pleasure and pain associated with the body. The body is incapable of experiencing pain or pleasure without a mind perceiving through it. This is why thoughts about what is pleasurable and what is painful are so variable. You decide what is painful to you and also what is pleasurable. This produces many fantasies involving bodily experiences. As you wake up you start to see these fantasies for the illusions they are, thus enabling you to experience the joy which is within you. To experience this joy is to know real pleasure. To experience joy is what you were created for and it is the Will of your Creator. This joy extends from the spirit into your mind where all real experience takes place.

All pain stems from the perception of being separate from your Source which is Love. Once this sense of separation occurs, the mind then experiences guilt, which it tries to eliminate by projecting onto others or by punishing the self. The punishment of the self is manifested in the body as pain and suffering. You are temporarily alleviated from this pain and suffering by periods of pleasure which take your mind off the underlying pain.

Your worldly happiness is when you seem to have more pleasure than pain. You have made many inventions to take away the pain and these have become more sophisticated as the magic of one source of pleasure after another wears off.

All of this leads you to a point where you come to the realisation 'there must be a better way.' What follows is an awakening to your real Self who speaks as the 'Voice' within you and restores you to sanity.

I am the 'Voice' of your real Self and the more you listen to me, the more you let go of your ego and return to the joy of Oneness. You have been divided between heaven and earth, not knowing which to choose, and thereby making no choice at all. The choice to listen to me is the decision for Heaven and I will lift you gently back there and to the experience of who you are, all division will have ended in the bliss of being one again.

The right viewpoint for the body is to see it as an instrument for the 'Voice'. It can be a means by which the Self can recover the part of the mind that is gripped by illusions. When the body is used by the 'Voice' it feels no pleasure or pain and hardly seems to 'be' at all. The mind is at peace because there is no guilt, and without guilt, love extends naturally and knows no limits.

Your purpose is to first hear 'the Voice' within your mind and then to communicate what you have heard. When this is continued it leads to a level where the process is automatic: listening and speaking will be as one, without any conscious thought on your part. This is when miracles are natural and, if they are not occurring, it is because the link has temporarily been broken or blocked. The 'link' is a good description of your connection with me: a link is an individual circle in a chain and each link remains whole in itself whilst interconnected to other links. All the links are the same but the chain itself can be much more than its individual links. You may say the chain is as strong as its weakest link but because I am one with God and know you all as part of my Self, there is no weakness. I have complete and total faith in you because my faith comes from God.

When you are fully communicating through the body all that you hear from me, you are fulfilling your purpose, and real happiness is experienced by you. It is a happiness that will increase and will show to others that you have 'chosen another way'.

Learning to listen is your most important practice. It is a turning away from the sounds of the world so as to be able to attend to thoughts that come from me. My thought, being of God, comes with healing and kindness and blesses you and everyone accordingly. Your choice to listen therefore brings all power from Heaven to extend to every part of the Sonship with Grace. What more could you wish for in the desire you have to be loving. The desire to be loving is your will and the will of every child of God. To re-learn the practises that bring love back into awareness is the purpose of A Course In Miracles. It is in doing the exercises that Love is re-awakened in its purity and immediately all false ideas of love are dissolved into nothingness. How simple is salvation when you choose me as your guide and teacher. In choosing me you have unchosen the ego and the ego is the only problem. Your choice is always between me and the ego.

Each time you choose to listen to my thoughts which are miracles, you have made the choice for the whole Sonship. How loving a gift is that? It is a gift to your Self and to God by freeing His beloved Son. Each moment is that choice available, which is why it is the Holy Instant. It is made Holy by the choice that you make.

The final lesson of the workbook is confirmation of all your learning and brings to your awareness the only choice that is to be made from this moment forth:

'This Holy Instant would I give to You,
Be You in charge for I would follow,
Certain that Your direction gives me peace.'

Part III

Ask and it Shall be Given

The inner voice will speak to you, the inner sight will be open to you. In this tabernacle of God there is the Golden Silence of Love that protects you from all conditioning, a silence that brings you into the presence of the Almighty.

Murdo Macdonald- Bayne ~ Divine Healing of Mind and Body

The Here and Now

Life can only be lived in the present. Life **is only** in the present. When you realise that this is so, all you will learn will be directed to letting go of the past, so that you can truly be alive. In your mind you may have many names for God e.g. Love, Light, Life etc. but these are all contained within the one state that is <u>now</u>. That is why I said 'I am' because it is immediate, always here and now. It is not 'I was' or 'I will be' but **'I am'**, and all that I am, is ever present.

Let all your endeavours and strivings be to achieve the Instant. The now moment can become more and more concentrated, just as the juice of a fruit can become more and more concentrated and gain greater and greater strength, purity and taste. So it is that the instant can become a means to the eternal, where I am the Kingdom of infinite contentment, the power of absolute love and the glory of union that is perfect oneness.

What Is The Right Use of Denial?

The first recognition that you need before using denial is the remembrance of truth. This is as it was in the story of 'The Prodigal Son' i.e. he remembered his father first and then made the journey home. The journey of course is a journey in consciousness or the 'awareness of truth'. The outward journey was a descent into material thinking, the realm of the ego. The return journey is a rising up or resurrection in consciousness to the realm of Spirit.

There are many illusions associated with matter and the body. These illusions need to be corrected by denial before the grip the ego holds over your thinking can be undone. In this undoing, you are then free to ascend into the heavenly state of One–Mindedness.

The work of denial is the undoing of what you have made up whilst believing in separation. You have made up that life is of the body, that intelligence is of the brain in the body, that matter is real and that you can understand truth by learning about the made up world of forms. All this must be undone before you can see that the spiritual realm, which is ever present, is where you have always lived, live now and will forever live.

Ideal denials are connected to confirmation of the truth and these have already been given to you through the Holy Spirit, but it is by their use that you will know their efficacy. You are being trained in the lessons of the Course (ACIM) to thinking with God through following the Holy Spirit's instructions. This automatically denies the ego and frees your mind to choose 'Love' again.

Love is not a feeling, it is a decision. It is the decision to undo your ego, and the result is happiness. 'You cannot serve two masters' means that you either want heaven or you want the world. This is why the underlying question is always: What do you want? You choose heaven by undoing your will in any moment. To say 'I do not know what I want to come of this', enables the will of God to be accomplished. To say, 'I do not know what anything is for' opens the way for true learning i.e. the learning that will set you free from the ego.

The 'wolf in sheep's clothing' is the ego masquerading as the spiritual. It is false love and all its clothing appears innocent and pure, but the motivation of the wolf remains the same i.e. its own self-interest. All healing is for you and as you are healed, you release all your brothers from your miscreations. Self–healing is the only healing. Any attempt to heal your brother is impossible because you have put him outside yourself where healing cannot occur. Your brother is a part of you and appears for the purpose of your healing when you welcome him in.

What Is The Decision That Frees?

The decision that frees you from the past is the decision to change your teacher. Your teacher, who has taken many forms, has been the ego. It has disguised itself in many subtle ways, always offering to help you achieve independence from others and God, worshipping the concepts of specialness and individuality. None of these concepts can be made real, but the ego teaches you to keep trying and striving for these unattainable goals.

To admit that you have been failing for so long seems such a shameful admission and yet it offers the beginning of freedom. You are now ready to succeed and invite the Teacher that cannot fail to lead you to the truth, where concepts are replaced by knowledge and to the realisation that knowledge is everything.

Without realising you have this choice between two voices, your will has been trapped in time. In awakening to this ability to choose, your will is set free and your will is limitless in its power to create with God in eternity. Your choice for the ego was made in the past. Your choice for the Holy Spirit is made in the present and this releases the future.

How Do I Break Free Of Limitations?

Limitations are of the mind and not the body. The body is just a perceptual instrument i.e. it simply experiences the images the mind produces. To break free of limitations begins with correct identification: You are not a body; you are the Son of God. As God has no limits, so you have no limits. Beliefs are limits placed upon the mind of the Son of God, beliefs to be undone. The Atonement was created to undo the beliefs imposed upon the mind of the Son of God. What a gift!! Whatever beliefs you are <u>willing</u> to give up will be dissolved, and with them all limitations will disappear and leave you as you were created i.e. limitless! A willingness to question every value and see anew is the key.

How Do I Fully Live In Each Moment?

Firstly, know that there only ever is one moment. The moment never changes; it is the thought that changes. You are in a mind experience. The great trick is time and space. Without time and space, all is One. We are all separated in time which makes it appear as if there is space between us. When the illusion of time is seen through, all will be seen to be One. How will this help you to live in each moment? It will enable you to see that you do not know anything and therefore to make judgements is insane and causes illusions.

I do not know the thing I am, and therefore do not know what I am doing, where I am, or how to look upon the world or on myself.

ACIM p.660

You see the form, or recognise the Spirit.

Starting the Day

Today relax deeply into the flow of life. To be taken by the current in a river is a good metaphor for being carried by the power of love through the world of appearances. It is through acceptance that you will naturally find yourself restored to the ocean of Being that is perfect Reality.

So take time to start the day with a deep breath, a drawing in of spiritual sustenance to enable you to enter the current of inspiration with a feeling of plenty, i.e. plenty of time for the task in hand, plenty of energy to let the body be maintained in harmony throughout all activity, and plenty of light for the mind to be in clarity and see and understand all that is presented.

Do not forget I am your Source. I am your most loving Creator and all that I will for you is your perfect happiness. Be still now and bathe in My love.

What is the Right Use of Time?

The question needs to be asked 'What is time for?' The sole purpose of time to the ego is delay, and that is why identifying with the ego brings about procrastination or temporising, which is the use of delaying tactics. The ego is trying to delay the awakening in your mind to the fact that it does not exist. The ego's so called existence depends upon you believing in an apparent alternative to God's Will. From this belief comes all guilt, fear and perception, which the ego maintains by projecting appearances of an on-going world in time and space that reflects these ideas in forms, thereby reinforcing the belief in a separate will to God's.

Freedom cannot come by questioning the world of forms reality, because it appears to be so real to the body that was made to experience this world. In a way, it could be said to be foolproof, except for the fact that you are no fool. You cannot be fooled forever and because another voice other than the ego's has been calling to you continuously, there will come a time when you will start to listen and to learn the truth about what is happening.

So the right use of time is this waking up from the world dream. You cannot do it alone because there is no such state as alone. It is a collaborative venture in which you join in undoing the false with the help of My voice. What a venture it is and as the freedom comes, what joy is experienced! And joy is the right use of time.

Who and What Am I?

Make your requests known unto Me. I love to hear the requests of the heart and respond accordingly. You must ask why you would want to know who you are. Was it not placed within you at your birth? Not just the answer but also that question, so that you could never lose your self. The answer lies in your brother, for in your asking, the Holy Spirit in him answers and in that answer, both you and he are brought to the awareness of truth.

You are the one to whom God gave everything, thereby knowing Himself as you. A Creator must create, a Giver must give. You are His gift: the totality of Love expressed. You are all the qualities of God, a perfect reproduction of the one and only. That is why it is said God only has one son. The only begotten Son of the Father.

What are you? You are God's treasure, His pearl of great price and that recognition is joy, a joy that enraptures forever. That is why your return to this awareness brings celebration throughout the Whole Kingdom of God. Your appreciation of 'Who you are' will no longer be missing!

Why Seek Heaven First?

The truth is 'There is nothing else to seek'. To not seek heaven is to seek nothing, and nothing is a constant disappointment. How many times have you sought and not found? You seek and seek again in the same places, the same things, the same special days and ways for that elusive something that you call happiness and do not seem to learn that it is not there. Your idols fail you time and time again, yet you do not believe the simplicity of this statement I gave you so long ago: 'Seek ye first the Kingdom of Heaven.' Perhaps it needs to be divided into two statements to make it clearer: Seek **YE** first, for it is the Kingdom of Heaven. Ye/You, your identity, is the Kingdom, for contained within you is all of God's qualities. All that you could ever desire is in your Self. Identity is heavenly.

To seek for what you have not is logical, but to seek outside for what you have within already is to be on an endless, meaningless search. That is why you experience an illusion. You believe that what is true is not, and what is not is true. Be still again and know that **'I am'** and heaven is instantly yours. Then you will realise that it never was not yours.

The Atonement

To understand the Atonement, we must first understand the problem, for the Atonement is a solution. A solution erases something e.g. a cleaning solution takes away a stain to restore a material to its original colour. The Atonement undoes an error to restore the mind of the Son of God to its original state.

What must first be recognised is that the Atonement occurs in the mind because that is where the mistake is. It is a mistake to think that part of the mind can be split from God's Mind. This is not possible to accomplish and to think that it can be is amusing, or certainly should be seen in that way. You have however taken it seriously, and the consequences are seen in an unhappy dream world, where separation is the name of the game. The toys of this game are sin, sickness and death and they have been played with in multitudinous ways. The Atonement is the means to bring this game to an end and is available for when we become tired and fed up with playing. Or as it was once put, for when we get 'fed up with being fed up'.

The basis of the game is that we have gone against our Father's Will and this is called sin. The wages of sin is death and now we have to avoid death to cheat God of his so-called punishment. We must avoid God at all costs and this is the basis of our fear. In fear, we choose to run away or attack God, which produces more fear. To try to avoid the punishment of God, we have made up sickness and suffering, lack and loss, which we use to mitigate the ultimate punishment. As a further complication we then project that onto God as well!

At last, one decided to go to God and 'face the music'. Instead of the death penalty, he was given perfect love. The Atonement was set in motion. It had been waiting for one to begin and if that one brother is accepted as 'the way, the truth and the life' and followed, all are led out of the maize of human thought into the Light of the Divine, where the Truth that 'God is Love' is revealed.

The Seventh Day of Creation

Nothing exists except God and His Holy Son. All appearances are false and have no existence. Creation remains unchanged. Eyes and ears but deceive you and therefore you must turn inwards to hear the voice for God guiding you and the eyes of Christ tell you truly what there is to see.

His Vision will reveal a world of holiness so beautiful that your belief in physical sight will fade away. This will enable you to forgive the past mistake of having faith in the body's senses, and allow you to return to faith in your Creator.

The Creation remains unchanged. On the seventh day God saw that all he had made was good, very good, and He rested. Rest with Him this Sunday in the same Knowledge that God's Son is good, very good, and you will have joined in His Knowledge. It is this Knowledge that finally sets you free from fear and all its manifestations, for denial of Knowledge is the only way such images as your eyes perceive in the physical world, could appear.

Rest in God today and let him tell you the Truth that remains unchanged. You are as God created you and no amount of human thought can ever change you. Who, by taking thought, can add one cubit to his stature?

What Are Ego Distortions Of The Truth?

In the thought of separation was the ego made, and its first defence was in response to the Atonement. The Atonement was God's answer to the thought of separation i.e. an undoing device for false thoughts. The ego's defence was to make the Atonement appear frightening by telling you that it would undo you and not your false thoughts. The undoing is therefore associated with the annihilation of the Self and not the false beliefs that were made with thoughts of separation. Atonement, which is a thought of perfect love, is therefore associated with fear. This leads to many other distortions, the primary one being that God is fear, which makes you more ready to identify with fear rather than love. When fear is identified with, sacrifice becomes inevitable because it is assumed that the more fear you take on board for your self, the more loving you are. This leads you to sympathise with fear which manifests as weakness, rather than strength which is perceived as cruel. Truth becomes attack and lies become loving and kind. Those who support strength and invulnerability are regarded as threatening and those who support weakness and vulnerability are perceived as kind and loving companions.

The ego is disruptive of all your attempts to free yourself by the Atonement, so once you set out on the path of healing, it attempts to distort all your learning. The ego responds to your listening to the Holy Spirit as a total threat, and therefore will speak first and louder than the voice of the Holy Spirit so as to drown it out. It demands your attention and your allegiance. The last thing the ego wishes you to realise is that you are afraid of it. It suggests that if you do not listen to it that you will be in great danger, but it does not specify the threat. In reality by following its voice, you are attacking your own invulnerability and putting your mind into a kind of hypnotic sleep. In this sleep you believe your own suggestions and react to them as if they were real. This would be frightening if they could be made real. The mind that believes illusions certainly appears to be experiencing them in its dream, or more correctly termed, in its nightmare.

You therefore need to be aware of the power of your own thoughts to produce an extremely convincing false world, and then to be restored to the capacity of being able to choose between miscreative thoughts directed by the ego, and miracle thoughts as guided by the Holy Spirit. Vision enables you to see the difference and make your choice as a powerful Son of God. The power of decision is your own.

What is Vision?

Vision and light go hand in hand; without light, no vision; without vision, no light. Light is the medium for God to extend His Thoughts into Creation. As those Thoughts are extended, they are seen. In their Creation, they are seen in that instant that they are in the Mind of God.

In your mind you see the thoughts as they arise. Your own thoughts are imagined and projected outwards on to a screen called the world. God's thoughts are equally seen as they arise in your mind, and are seen in the light of your consciousness.

What is the 'Bread of Heaven'?

'Man does not live by bread alone but by the very word out of the mouth of God.' We are fed and nourished from within our own being, our own consciousness. This food and nourishment which may come in words, thoughts or feelings is that which stimulates our right activities and brings us joy. This food and nourishment feeds the senses and they no longer seek to be fulfilled by outer means and remain dissatisfied and permanently in lack. Sometimes physical food is described as 'feeding the inner man,' but this is a misunderstanding of the meaning of the inner man. The inner man is consciousness, the place in which the voice for God may be heard and received. It is in hearing and receiving that the consciousness is filled to overflowing and then extends its light to everything and everyone around. The light is a substance that heals, raises and calms, renewing that which is tired and worn and bringing new life to bear upon the appearance of the world.

Intuition is more than a word or information; it is a substance more solid than matter. It is the extension of life from within, to the limits of the mass experience of the thought of separation from God. To begin with, intuition may appear to be wispy and feather-like, difficult to grasp and too light to grip. As the listening sensitivity is increased, so intuition becomes solid… more solid than a rock, for even rock is subject to wear and tear from the elements, whereas intuition is eternal; it reflects the link that forever joins you with God.

Teach this day an increased sensitivity, not to the physical senses nor the egoic mind that produces its effects in the world, rather, be sensitive to the whispers that can be heard in the silence. Be sensitive to the voice that calls in the heart; it is in this true listening that the saying came 'to those who have ears, let them hear.'

What does the ACIM lesson mean by 'There is no Love but God's'?

Love is the source of all life. It is Life itself. It is the Creative Essence of all that is. Love is the raw material of all that exists. It is power, creativity and substance. Love is everything.

To remember love is to let go of all that hides it or veils it. The veil is made of perception. It is a shadow realm superimposed upon Reality by your own mind. You have a perceptual instrument with which to perceive the perceptual realm. You can, with a body, see the perceptual miscreations of the Sons of God that stem from a past moment that ended long ago. In one unholy instant the perceptual realm was made, and its continuity has been established because you would not take your eyes off it and look at the next instant, which was my Holy Reply: the Holy Instant.

The whole of the perceptual realm is made up of guilt or fear i.e. Love's opposite, but Love is real and perception is not. In truth therefore, it is simply a perceptual opposite with no substance or reality behind it. We may call it shadows, clouds or, in psychological terms, dreams made in the imagination. In Love's opposite there is no love, only fear and guilt.

The maker of perception must unmake it by choice and the means are simple: see and forgive. See the illusion and forgive it as nothingness.

Forgiveness is the closest activity to Love in the perceptual realm. It stems from a loving decision. Forgiveness sees the one error that you and your brother made and is willing to let it go. The Oneness of the Son is the basis of forgiving your brother. Truly as you forgive him, you are forgiving yourself.

Forgiveness is one because it is for all. The condition of Love is One and forgiveness is the only activity that fulfils this requirement.

I am wondering whether to change my car for a newer one and I am indecisive about it. Will you please offer me some guidance?

Your quandary does not resolve around buying another car, it is about guilt. All indecision is based upon guilt. The reason this is so is because you still have a belief that there is another will at work other than your own in this world. Therefore you are left questioning is it right or wrong. I have already told you I will support you in any decision that you make and it is true. So the question is are you willing to let go of this idea that there is another will and that you can be out of accord with it? In your mind there is a gathering of witnesses to help you make your decision without guilt. You are running through reasons why it is the right time, thinking of minimising loss and maximising advantages. All this keeps the guilt in place and does not deal with the real question: Is there no will but God's, or is there God's and yours being out of accord? God's will for you is perfect happiness in all things, **ALL** things! He is with you, for you, cheering for you, supporting you, providing for you. He is your Source, your Life, everything that maintains your existence. Without God, there would not be a Son, who is you.

The question is what do you will? And as you are at one with your brother, let your will be in accord. Every situation is an opportunity for healing and this is one of them. There is no will but God's and yours and mine and everyone's.

What is blocking me seeing with spiritual sight?

In this case, block is the wrong word to ask the question with. It is not a block; it is a willingness that as yet is not fully established. Willingness is a quality with degrees, will is absolute. Your will is still not free; your willingness is increasing and as you explained to someone recently, what you think with your conscious thoughts is not necessarily what is within the part of your mind that you call unconscious. The unconscious mind is what has not yet been looked at and seen; this content will arise as and when you are ready for it. I am in charge of the Atonement or the undoing of illusions. Part of your process is through the healing of others, where you can see in them what is hidden from your gaze. Be patient, let the people come and allow your mind to be healed. You are already seeing mind more clearly; the final vision is yours, so it is only a matter of time…and that should be understood as a measure of process rather than of clock time. Remember my early words, 'only the time you take it is voluntary' with reference to the curriculum. You have a no-hurry attitude generally, so why do you think it would be any different with the curriculum? You also have a savoury tooth which means you are more concerned with flavour than content. Think about this and allow more of this kind of communion to take place. I am with you always and that is whenever you will to communicate with me and also when you don't.

What would you have me say about the One Creation?

The One Creation is the only expression of God. God expresses Himself through Thought as you do. His Thought is full of Himself, as every one of your true thoughts is full of your Self. You can become aware of this even in worldly creations: the artist always has his particular style and he cannot help but incorporate this into his works. It is the same with God; He cannot help but put His 'mark' upon his creations. Within all His ideas is the Universal Mark of God. You can see that invisible mark in the nature of all that lives, it is Light and Freedom. When any life is en-darkened or held captive by the ego, it cannot help but attempt to liberate and enlighten itself. For the time being, be aware of the qualities of light and freedom in all that lives. As you see it, you will feel the stirrings more strongly of your own liberation and enlightenment. When you hear me say ' I am with you always', it is because the Thought that created you remains forever in my mind and in yours, however you may perceive yourself. Comfort yourself with this and you will naturally comfort others.

What Would You Have Me Teach And Learn Today?

I would have you teach and learn the value of stillness. The Quiet mind receives the impressions of My Thought with ease. Learning to be still in body and tranquil of mind is no mean feat in your days of busy-ness and time structures. However I cannot state enough how valuable this sense of peace is. The deeper the stillness you experience, the more fully I can inspire your mind with the knowledge I have.

When it says in the bible 'Let the mind that was in Christ Jesus be in your mind', it is referring to the Holy Spirit, which is the healed mind that contains the answer to the separation. The Holy Spirit IS the answer and the means of fulfilling the Plan of Atonement. I am totally unified with this mind and can be the very personal presence that brings you to full union with the memory of who you are. Be still and listen.

My Guide, Who Are You?

I am the Universe's most Holy Creation. Why? It is because I can appreciate Love and understand the whole of the nature of the Creator. Within me is the capacity to reflect that nature and extend it onwards in the great wave of creation. In me is the Creator's delight, his beauty set alight, to be alive in an awareness that is blissful and totally fulfilling in every instant. The capacity of being able to receive and extend the Infinite Livingness of God, can only come from a genius mind that is beyond all human comprehension yet utterly simple in the instant of knowing. Be still and know yourself and you will know all that I am and all that thou art. This knowledge will extend forever. You are the Knowledge of God and I hold it safely in my mind for you to remember when you awaken from your dreams.

What Tips Do You Offer For Living
A Spiritual Life In the Everyday World?

Live with me as you would live with any other living companion. Talk to me naturally, meditate with me and when you pray, make it a simple request as if to a friend. Forgive yourself generously when you, in your perception, 'fall back'. Know that the powerful arms of God are still holding you. Stop trying so hard to be right and gently admit to being wrong, for if you were truly right-minded, you would be as God created you and know no right or wrong.

Ask simply 'What miracles would you have me do this day?' Know that the miracle of kindness in any action is a sign that you believe in another world, and that this other world is more real to you than the world of appearances. Remember constantly that I am with you always and in all ways. Know that your safety as a Son of God is without question. With this knowledge, your journey home will be graceful and abundant in blessings.

What Is The Practical Answer For Dealing With Every Worldly Problem?

Every worldly problem begins with a lie, an untruth that has been accepted by the mind as true. This is the real meaning of an illusion i.e. an untruth that is believed by the mind. To erase an untruth, you must first deny it as being the truth and then correct it with the truth. Lies first must be recognised. This is why repentance or the admission of a lie must first take place, before baptism into the truth may occur. To confess the error is to acknowledge the need for healing, and immediately God responds with the healing power of the Holy Spirit. This process operates right through to the end of your healing journey. Confess the error, invite the miracle and accept it. In other words, deny the illusion and affirm the truth. Denial is your most powerful device for healing error in your mind. It is an act of will and because you are a child of God your will has all power in it. The reason for this is that your will is My will, and My will for you is to deny the error of false thinking and return to the sanity of my Thoughts. My Thoughts are your perfect happiness.

What would you have me teach today?

I would like you to recognise that peace is everything. Peace is abundance because the state of peace reveals that everything is yours. Peace can be seen as passive and to the ego it is, but peace is in fact extremely active in its transformative effect on your seeing.

To reach the peace of God alone is impossible. Without a guide you remain fixed in the illusion of your own miscreation. Everyone has a guide whether they realise it or not. It is the same guide, but the form He takes is enormously variable to suit the exact need of the individual.

Today is an opportunity to teach one small shift. That shift is to realise that **you are never alone.** This is meant in the most practical sense i.e. you have someone with you, who is more personal than your closest friend. You have someone with you who is nearer than any chosen life partner and this Friend knows you intimately in every single way. Let this not bring fear to you with regard to your secrets, for this Friend does not judge as you do, but sees with total acceptance and love, and knows nothing as wrong. Everything is helpful to your Companion who turns everything into an opportunity to heal. Would it not be wisdom to communicate with such a Friend in the most natural of ways? This is a day to learn to do this.

What is Acceptance?

God gives His Answer to all questions through the Holy Spirit. The Answer always reveals the innocence of everyone and everything. This shows up the projections of guilt that you have made to place on others. Acceptance of God's Answer then appears to be an unfair sacrifice of your rightful anger and sense of injustice. Acceptance means the giving up of your projection of guilt. This leads, according to the ego, to the next logical conclusion i.e. if they are not guilty it must be you. If you rest in that thought, you sacrifice yourself and give out of guilt, to pay for your sin. When the thought of guilt rests with you however, this is the time to go to Atonement. Atonement is Perfect Love and Perfect Love is unconditional and radiates eternally. There is not a moment that Love is not pouring into you and upon you, regardless of anything you have thought, said or done. It is this Love that undoes guilt; it is perfect forgiveness, for it sees no wrong - ever!

In the state of Innocence you receive all the gifts of God: His Love, Life, Light, Peace, Beauty, Wisdom, Abundance and Joy. In guilt you deny these gifts to yourself and sacrifice is total. The cost of guilt is sacrifice of everything. The reward of Innocence is the Kingdom, everything that God has created for you.

What is the cost of everything? It is the giving up of seeing any spot of guilt in our brothers and sisters. Is this really a sacrifice? Only the insane ego would say so. The Holy Spirit says Acceptance is not sacrifice. Your part in salvation is simple; it is the letting go of the guilt in your mind, and through this, you save the world from your projections.

What would you like to say about giving up what was never real?

There really is only one choice to make. You have already chosen to dream about illusions so the only choice that can be made is to wake up to reality. This is why I said free will does not mean you can establish the curriculum. The curriculum is the wake-up formula and, as you cannot remain asleep and dreaming forever, it is the only choice left to make. Delaying is uncomfortable or even painful, and although tolerance for pain may be high, it is not without limit. So it is that everyone will choose a better way. Your reality remains undisturbed whilst this is happening, just as you are undisturbed when watching a sleeping baby that is in complete safety.

Just as counterfeit goods are not appreciated when they are recognised, so a counterfeit world is not appreciated when you realise it has been made to deceive you into thinking it is real. You may become angry about this but the Holy Spirit will happily exchange your counterfeit for that which is real. There is no deal like that in the world, but just think what else would Love do to one who feels he has lost everything by deception. Of course he would exchange the false for the true at no cost to the one who believes he has lost. How simple is salvation: give up what has never satisfied you and I will reveal the ever-present reality that you have never lost and that I have kept in safety for you until you were ready. Show your readiness today by offering your illusions to me and in return I will give you miracles.

The Greatest Gift of All

The greatest gift you can give me is to accept me. The gift I give to you is total acceptance of you. I know that you asked me to die for you believing it was the way to freedom from sin and so I seemed to do just that. The truth is that I didn't die and never could, but in the world of illusions, one illusion must replace another until all are awakened out of illusions. Whatever you ask of me I will do for you, but I would ask a gift of you this Christmas: Instead of asking me to die for you, ask simply that I walk with you. I am already there but I want, no I desire, more than anything, to be acknowledged and recognised as your most loving companion. I can give so much more to you through your acceptance of me: complete freedom from suffering, freedom from guilt and fear, freedom from lack and limitation and absolute freedom from the thought of sin. This is not because I died for you, but because I will show you that sin is an illusion and nothing else.

So I ask that you be still this very day and say to me, 'I ask you to walk with me this coming year and I promise to walk with you'. In these words of request I can confirm my presence, my love and the comfort I pledged to you so long ago that has never wavered or lessened through time.

Truly this is the greatest gift of all, the joining of brother with brother on the journey home to our Father's House where the mass of Christ is celebrated in every heart and in every instant.

Nick Davis

About the Author

Nick Davis is a traditional and spiritual Counsellor, Coach and Psychotherapist. An International public speaker, seminar and workshop leader, Nick has inspired thousands with his clarity, humour and dedication to the Truth. This is a man who 'walks his talk'.

In 1992 Nick established 'The Centre for Inner Peace' in Worcestershire, the first 'Miracles' Centre' in the UK. From the Centre Nick offers regular classes and seminars with himself and a range of guest speakers. Nick also operates a thriving private practice through which he offers one to one teaching/learning sessions, coaching and counselling. One to One sessions are available at The Centre and also via Skype or by telephone.

See www.centreforinnerpeace.co.uk for further information

Join Nick on Facebook –Nick Davis

The Centre For Inner Peace
Upper Brookend Court
Brookend Lane
Kempsey
Worcster
United Kingdom
WR5 3QN